Small Wonders

Jean-Henri Fabre & His World of Insects

Small

Wonders

Jean-Henri Fabre & His World of Insects

Matthew Clark Smith
illustrated by Giuliano Ferri

two lions

Once there was a village in the sunny south of France: a village much like any other, where the cocks crowed and the church bells rang, and everyone seemed to know his or her place. Everyone, that is, but one.

At the very edge of town, behind high walls and plane trees, there stood a pink house. In the house lived an old man with beetle-black eyes and a black felt hat who talked to animals. Whether he was a sorcerer, or simply a madman, no one could agree.

On the hottest afternoons, he squatted in the sun, watching beetles dig holes.

On the darkest nights, he crouched in the bushes watching spiders build webs.

He paid the village children to find dead moles and lizards for a penny apiece; then he set them out in the garden to lure bluebottle flies.

Inside the house, according to rumor, lurked even stranger things. Scorpions scuttling in cages. Swallows darting through open windows. Pickled sea creatures arriving in crates. And roasted caterpillars—one man swore it—for dinner! Over the years the old man's reputation grew and grew, cocooned in mystery.

And then, one bright fall day when the old man was very old indeed, the villagers heard the strange *chug-chug-chug* of motorcars in the valley.

The cars, sleek and black, rumbled up to the pink house in a swirl of dust. A figure stepped out, and then another figure with a familiar face. It was the President of France!

The villagers whispered and stared. Who was this man, this mysterious neighbor, who spoke to presidents and beetles alike?

His name was **Jean-Henri Fabre**.

There are many paths to genius. Monsieur Fabre's had begun on the side of a mountain, nearly a century before.

Little Henri lived in an old gray farmhouse that was the only house for miles. In fact, it was the only anything for miles, other than the pigs and cows that trudged through the bogs, the potatoes that strained against the stony soil, and the gorse bushes that clung to the rocks. After dark, Henri fell asleep to the whipping of the wind and the howling of wolves.

But where others might have seen a harsh, gray world—a world of rocks and bogs, cow dung and rain—Henri saw a world of small wonders.

Here was a sky-blue jewel on the bottom of a leaf—or so it seemed.

Here was a hen's egg in moss, round and white, yet soft as a pillow.

Here was a tiny ram's horn carved in stone.

Here were diamonds and gold dust, treasures locked in the hollows of pebbles.

Only later would he learn the real names of these things and repeat them to himself like magic charms: **Hoplia beetle. Amanita mushroom. Ammonite fossil. Quartz crystals** and **mica flakes.**

For now, they were nameless miracles.

When Henri was seven years old, his family moved into town and he started school. Still, he found marvels everywhere. When his father sent him to mind the ducks at the pond, Henri came back soaking wet, his pockets sagging with treasures.

While his classmates scribbled their lessons in Latin, Henri fiddled with wasp stingers and snapdragon pods, hidden in the nooks of his desk.

Mostly, he kept these things to himself. No one else seemed to understand. What good, demanded his teacher, could ever come of squinting at flowers when there was Greek and arithmetic still to master?

Henri's father moved the family from town to town, searching for a better life that seemed forever out of reach.

By the time Henri turned sixteen, he decided to strike out on his own. He joined a railroad crew, sold lemons at a market, and lived sometimes on little more than grapes snatched from roadside vineyards.

And yet everywhere he looked, small wonders called to him. Every patch of dirt and tangle of weeds buzzed with insects: dazzling beetles, ferocious wasps, sweet-singing crickets, and more.

At last Henri found a job as a teacher, but the classroom was dark and clammy. He took his students outside, where they learned the songs of grasshoppers and drank honey from the clay nests of mason bees.

However, Henri soon realized that he now had little time to study his beloved insects. For years nothing seemed to come easy, except for one great happiness: he fell in love and married a young teacher named Marie. But their first two children died, and, exhausted by grief, Henri felt his insects slipping away.

Still he pressed on with his studies, finally earning the highest degree possible. And then one winter evening, Henri read an article that would rekindle his greatest passion.

It told of a certain wasp, the **Cerceris**, that hunted beetles nearly twice its own size. Each mother wasp left a beetle in her burrow along with her eggs, a meal for her children-to-be.

The beetle was dead—or so it seemed—yet however long it lay in that burrow, it stayed fresh. Had the wasp mastered the secret of preserving life beyond death?

Henri had read books about insects before, but they were dull beyond measure. Now his curiosity caught fire all over again. What about the lives of these animals—lives full of drama and mystery?

So he went out to stalk the Cerceris. He dug up the wasps' burrows, gathered beetles by the hundreds, brought them home to poke and prod. He spent hours bent in the grass watching the wasps hunt. And at last he arrived at an answer.

The beetles weren't dead at all. They were simply paralyzed, made forever still by one well-aimed stab from the wasp's venom-tipped stinger. When the baby wasps hatched, they ate their giant meal–alive!

Henri's findings caused a stir among his fellow scientists. It was hard to say which was more startling: the discovery itself, or the unknown outsider who had made it.

Eager to share what he'd learned, Henri taught classes for anyone who was interested. But when the authorities found out what he was teaching, they were not pleased. The bloodthirsty exploits of ant warriors? The secret love life of plants? Before he knew it, Henri was out of a job.

The next few years were dark ones. And one harsh winter, Henri caught a fearsome case of pneumonia. Shivering in bed, he was struck by a dreadful thought: he was going to die.

But he could not bear to go without saying good-bye to his beloved insects. He told his son of a colony of bees nearby, fast asleep in their winter nests. Soon the boy was back with a handful of bees, still as stones. He laid them out on his father's bed.

Just as Henri moved to touch them, he saw a sudden twitch. Then another. The bees were stirring, brought to life by the heat of the fire. They fluttered their wings, stretched their legs, wiggled their antennae. Before long they were buzzing at the windows!

Henri's heart leapt at the sight. Here was a reason to live. The insects needed a champion, someone to reveal their secrets to the world.

In the weeks and months that followed,
Henri began to write like a man possessed.
His words often flowed and danced like poems.
He wrote of the **Great Peacock**, the bat-winged
moth with what seemed like a sixth sense.
Henri combed almond twigs for the
moths' cocoons; he kept each cocoon
in a jar until the moth emerged.

If it was a female, a marvelous thing would happen. At night, called by some trace of a scent, male moths from miles around would be drawn to the female in the jar.

He wrote of the **Processionary**, that humble caterpillar that traveled in great caravans, end to end, day into night. Henri found he could place a line of caterpillars on the rim of a flowerpot, connect the back of the line to the front, and watch the creatures march in circles for days.

He wrote of the Empusa, or **Devilkin**, that strange and fierce-looking insect, with its great spike-lined claws and its warrior's headdress. To his surprise, Henri found it a delicate creature, very choosy about its meals.

And he wrote of the **Sisyphus**, the tiny dung beetle with what seemed like a model marriage. Henri watched each pair as it rolled a ball of dung, precious food for its babies, back to the nest. The beetles might work for hours—the female pulling, the male pushing from behind.

Henri wrote about dozens of other insects as well, each with its own fascinating story to tell. And as the years passed, word slowly spread of this curious hermit with the golden pen.

Eventually Henri had enough money to fulfill his oldest dream. He and his family found a tiny village with a pink house, tucked away behind high walls and plane trees, that seemed just right. It was here that he set about building his insects' paradise.

As Henri worked, the seasons passed: each season, and each year, brought new marvels. But did others see these things—really see them—as he did?

This is what Henri asked himself as he neared his ninetieth year. Looking back on his difficult life, he saw it as a small flower coaxed from stony soil. If his books had lit even the tiniest spark of wonder in one reader's heart, he thought, then perhaps he had been of some use.

It was then that the news came. The leading scientists in France had gathered to nominate one of their own for a tremendous honor. The vote had been unanimous. Jean-Henri Fabre, the insects' poet, was to be put forward for a Nobel Prize! Now, thought the committee: where can we find this man, this hidden treasure?

And so it was that the farmers of the little village of Serignan turned from their fields to discover a once-in-a-lifetime sight:

the President of France's gleaming motorcade, roaring down their dusty street.

One by one, the villagers dropped what they were doing. They ran toward the pink house . . .

. . . just in time to see their madman, their sorcerer, receiving his guest like a king.

We have all of us, men and animals, some special gift.
One child takes to music . . . another is quick with figures.
It is the same way with insects.
One kind of Bee can cut leaves, another builds clay houses. . . .
In human beings, we call the special gift genius.
In an insect, we call it instinct. Instinct is the animal's genius.

— *Jean-Henri Fabre*

Historical Note

When Jean-Henri Casimir Fabre was growing up in the early 1800s, scientists often studied plants and animals in laboratories or in distant, exotic places. Entomology, the study of insects, was considered to be of interest only to specialized experts. Of course, ordinary people were familiar with a handful of common "bugs" such as bees, crickets, or butterflies; but most books about entomology had little to do with insects like these. Instead, they were full of measurements and dry physical descriptions, often in Greek or Latin. Or they might be full of beautiful paintings, but the insects in these paintings—dead, preserved, and arranged in neat little rows—would be from faraway places.

Fabre was different. He wanted to study the insects he saw all around him, in the gardens and pastures and on the roadsides of rural France. And he wanted to study their behavior in life, instead of dissecting and comparing them after they died.

By watching insects carefully in their natural habitat, Fabre made important discoveries. He was the first to prove that insects used chemical scents called pheromones to communicate with each other. He was the first to figure out a process called hypermetamorphosis, which causes certain insects such as bee flies and blister beetles to take multiple distinct forms during their growth into adulthood. And he was the first to fully understand how instincts—"hard-wired" behaviors that an animal is born with—can explain so many of the amazing feats of insects, from a wasp paralyzing its beetle prey to a termite colony building a gigantic mound.

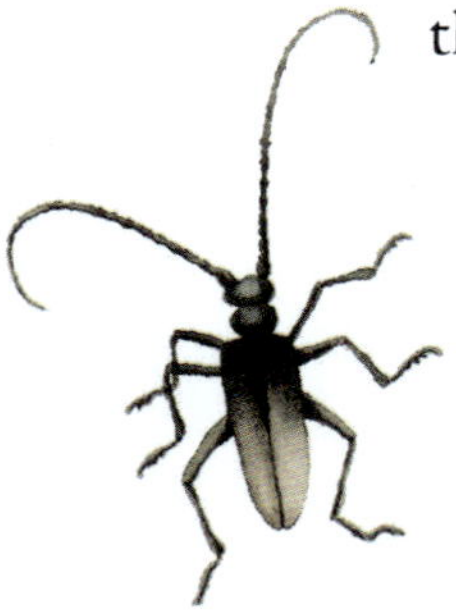

Not all of Fabre's findings have stood the test of time as well as these. But those who have followed in his footsteps have often pointed to him as a model of careful observation and experimentation. The great biologist Charles Darwin admired Fabre and called him "that inimitable observer."

Fabre accomplished many new and important things as a scientist. But what set him apart even more was his passion for sharing his observations with others—not just with the academic community, but with the wider world. Because he didn't shrink from any aspect of plant and animal life in his teachings and writings, and because some of his discoveries could seem unpleasant or even shocking, Fabre's contemporaries sometimes felt the need to shelter ordinary citizens—especially women and children—from his work. But Fabre believed that it was important for everyone to see nature in all its complexity. That included his own family, who supported him through times of hardship and doubt, and who often pitched in to help collect beetles, tend the garden, or feed the many creatures Fabre had brought home.

Fabre published more than two hundred works, ranging from technical reports to collections of poetry, and near the end of his life he became one of very few scientists ever to be nominated for a Nobel Prize in Literature. Many readers consider his masterpiece to be the *Souvenirs entomologiques* (Entomological Memories), ten books of essays on insects and other natural subjects, written in language that is both beautiful and easy to understand. These books, along with Fabre's other works, amount to a passionate plea to all of us to see the world through fresh, patient eyes—to appreciate the mystery and wonder of even the smallest creatures.

Today, most people know little about Fabre's life and work. He is best known in his native France, where his childhood home is now a museum alongside an insect-themed park and education center called Micropolis, and his pink house and gardens in Serignan have been restored and opened to the public. Nearly two hundred years after Fabre's birth, the world is changing much faster than the one he knew. Many of his beloved insects, along with so many other animals and plants, are threatened with extinction. His message has never been more important.

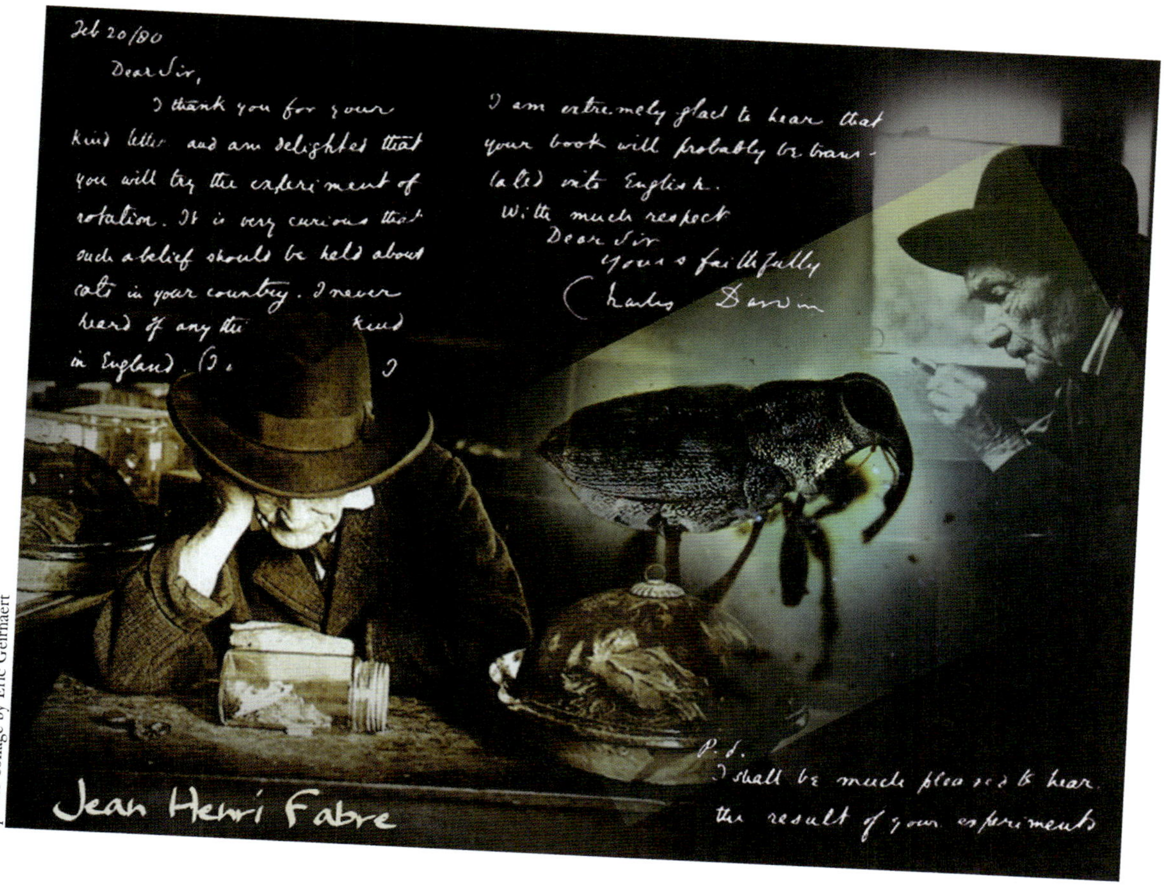

photo collage by Eric Geirnaert

Timeline

1823 Jean-Henri Casimir Fabre is born in Saint-Leons, France.
1826 Fabre is sent to live with his grandparents in the village of Malaval.
1828 The first railroad in France is built.
1830 Back in Saint-Leons, Fabre begins his schooling.
1832 The Fabres move to the larger town of Rodez, where Henri's father opens a café.
1838 Samuel Morse gives the first public demonstration of his telegraph machine.
1839 Fabre leaves school and strikes out on his own.
1842 Fabre graduates from teaching school and takes his first job at Carpentras.
1844 Fabre marries a fellow teacher, Marie-Césarine Villard.
1848 A revolution in Paris brings Louis-Napoleon (Napoleon III) to power.
1849 Fabre moves to the island of Corsica, where he finds a new job as a physics teacher.
1853 Fabre returns from Corsica, and begins teaching at a high school in Avignon.
1855 Fabre publishes his first scientific paper, on the Cerceris wasp and its weevil prey.
1859 Publication of Charles Darwin's *On the Origin of Species*.
1865 End of the American Civil War.
1866 Fabre is appointed curator of Avignon's natural history museum, and begins giving evening courses for adults.
1870 The popularity of Fabre's classes arouses suspicion, and he is forced to resign. The Fabres move from Avignon to the city of Orange.
1876 Alexander Graham Bell invents the telephone.
1877 Fabre's beloved son Jules dies at the age of sixteen.
1878 Fabre catches pneumonia and nearly dies.
1879 The Fabres move to the village of Serignan and buy a property called the Harmas, which Fabre begins converting into an "earthly paradise" for insects. Committed to the writing life, Fabre begins his greatest work, the *Souvenirs entomologiques*.
1889 The Eiffel Tower is built in Paris.
1903 The Wright brothers fly the first airplane.
1912 Fabre is nominated for the Nobel Prize in Literature.
1913 The President of France, Raymond Poincaré, visits Fabre at the Harmas.
1914 Outbreak of World War I.
1915 Fabre dies at the age of ninety-two.

Author's Note

When I started writing this book, I'd been an amateur naturalist and a bug lover for nearly my whole life. I'd studied biology in school, and I'd worked in environmental science for years after that. And yet I knew next to nothing about Jean-Henri Fabre. In fact, I might never have known much about him, if I hadn't noticed something odd in my garden one day: a dainty red-and-black wasp, slowly dragging a very large caterpillar across a flower bed. Where was it going? How did it know how to get there? Was the caterpillar dead? I was very curious but also very busy, so I left the wasp to its business and later followed up on this strange phenomenon in the usual way: I looked it up on the Internet.

A few hours later, I had learned several startling things: this man Fabre had answered all these very same questions, and he had done it about a hundred and fifty years ago without the Internet, or anything else except his two eyes and a few basic tools that you or I could probably make ourselves. I found this both inspiring and confusing. How did a simple farm boy, with very little in the way of money or equipment or reputation, become one of the most important scientists in the world? And why had I never learned about this man? Now I had more questions, and I soon realized that they—and their answers—added up to a book. I hope that *Small Wonders* helps, in some way, to spread Fabre's legacy as far and wide as he deserves.

Sources

Fabre, Jean-Henri. *The Insect World of Jean-Henri Fabre.* Trans. Alexander Teixeira de Mattos. Boston: Beacon Press, 1991. A sampling of essays from the *Souvenirs entomologiques* compiled and introduced by the great naturalist Edwin Way Teale. This book serves as a good introduction to Fabre's masterpiece.

Fabre, Augustin. *The Life of Jean Henri Fabre*. Trans. Bernard Miall. New York: Dodd, Mead & Co., 1921.

Legros, Georges Victor. *Fabre, Poet of Science*. Trans. Bernard Miall. London: T. Fisher Unwin, 1913. These two biographies are the only full-length biographies of Fabre that have been translated into English.

Raffles, Hugh. *Insectopedia*. New York: Vintage, 2001. This unique book contains an anthropologist's wide-ranging thoughts on insects' roles in human culture. The brief section on Fabre discusses his influence on modern science and natural history.

Acknowledgments:
Special thanks to Eric Geirnaert; photo collage image of Jean-Henri Fabre on page 41 © Eric Geirnaert

Published by Two Lions, New York
www.apub.com

The illustrations are rendered in watercolor and pencil.

Book design by Tanya Ross-Hughes
Editor: Melanie Kroupa

ISBN-13: 9781503949409 (paperback)
ISBN-10: 1503949400 (paperback)
Library of Congress Control Number: 2014915911

For Simon

—M.C.S.

To all who see the universe in
a single small wonder

—G.F.

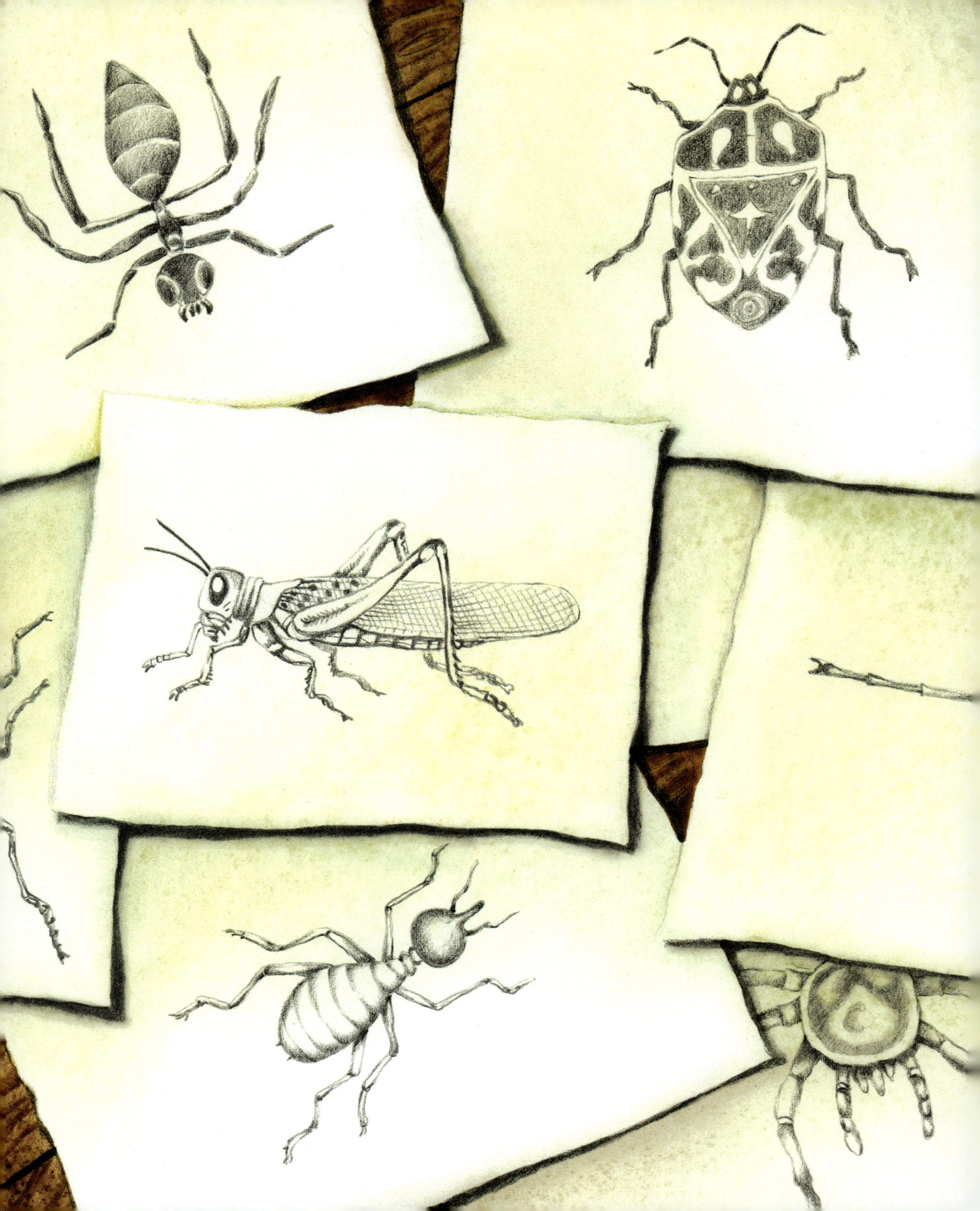

MATTHEW CLARK SMITH has been an amateur naturalist and lover of insects for nearly his whole life, having studied biology in school and worked in environmental science since then. He's also a designer, musician, and mapmaker, and recently earned a graduate degree in creative writing from Vermont College of Fine Arts. He lives in Jackson, Mississippi, with his family, where, he says, you have little choice but to come to terms with bugs. *Small Wonders* is his first children's book.

GIULIANO FERRI is a prize-winning illustrator and animator whose picture books have been published throughout the world. Like Jean-Henri Fabre, as a boy he, too, loved to lie in the grass to watch insects and discover the secret world hiding under his feet. Giuliano Ferri lives in Pesaro, Italy, with his family.

Printed in Great Britain
by Amazon

54645174R00028